22 Jun

012

Dear Keri

Wishing you Continued blessings
on your life,
   May His goodness and mercy
flow & follow you as promised
in Ps. 23.

with love
   Harriet xx.

# TRULY AMAZING!
## Encounters with Jesus

Andrew Feakin

**MOORLEY'S** Print & Publishing

British Library Cataloguing in Publication Data.
A catalogue record for this book is available
from the British Library.


ISBN 0 86071 558 2

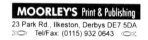

MOORLEY'S Print & Publishing
23 Park Rd., Ilkeston, Derbys DE7 5DA
Tel/Fax: (0115) 932 0643

# Contents

**Page**

1.  Introduction - Including 'The Gift of the Holy Spirit' (Poem)   4
2.  If Jesus walked the Earth today would He have a Mobile phone?   7
3.  Is your Line busy? (Poem)   9
4.  More than a Conqueror   10
5.  We live in an ever changing World   12
6.  God unchanging (Poem)   14
7.  Jesus changes Water to Wine   15
8.  The New Wine (Poem)   17
9.  He came by Night (Including Poem)   19
10. The Meeting   23
11. Take Time to Listen (Poem)   26
12. Jesus Heals the Official's Son   27
13. Your Son will Live (Poem)   28
14. The Healing at the Pool (Including Poem)   30
15. A very Special Day   34
16. Our Resources   36
17. The Woman caught in Adultery (Including Poem)   37
18. If you are Willing, you can Make me Clean   40
19. A Man with Leprosy (Poem)   42
20. An Encounter with a Greek Woman   43
21. The Faith of a Greek Woman (Poem)   45
22. The Healing of a Deaf and Mute Man   46
23. He has done Everything Well (Poem)   48
24. A Blind Man Healed at Bethsaida (Including Poem)   49
25. The Rich Young Ruler   52
26. "One thing you Lack" The Lordship of Jesus Christ (Poem)   54
27. The Widow's Mite   55
28. She gave all (Poem)   57
29. The Widow at Nain (Including Poem)   58
30. Jesus Anointed by a Sinful Woman   61
31. At the House of Simon (Poem)   64
32. "Bring the Boy to me"   65
33. The Healing of a Boy with an Evil Spirit (Poem)   66
34. Healing on the Sabbath (Including Poem)   69
35. I Want to See (Including Poem)   72
36. Ten Healed – One Saved (Poem)   76
37. Jesus and the Tax Collector   78
38. Today Salvation has come to this House (Poem)   80
39. The Parable of the Lost Son   81
40. The Homecoming (Poem)   83

# INTRODUCTION

Following on from being baptised and confirmed in March I became a Christian in June 1979. Attending Confirmation Classes had brought to me a greater awareness of God and His teachings but I still felt a degree of emptiness inside.

When the Confirmation classes ended the Vicar felt moved to try and keep the groups going but in a different form. Everyone including the recently confirmed was invited to Prayer and Praise Evenings to be held on Friday evenings at the Vicarage.

It was at one such meeting in June that I got a picture of a motorway before it was opened – before the tape that would open it to traffic had been cut. I found myself saying I want to feel absolutely free like that motorway with nothing in the way. God knew the cry of my heart. A short time elapsed which was probably only a matter of seconds and then two or three people just gathered round and prayed for me. I suddenly felt released within and that nothing was now in the way. I went home a different person, to my wife's surprise, and gradually I found my whole outlook on life changing and certainly my priorities.

Towards the end of 1979, however, I was experiencing a growing frustration, as I just seemed unable to successfully communicate this new life within me to others. How I wanted to get over the difference Jesus can make to your life.

At the beginning of January 1980 I earnestly prayed to God that He would use me in some way to spread His gospel.

One day in February I was just sat at my desk (I had just received an office of my own) at work when something truly amazing happened. I just felt as though a river was washing over me touching me from head to toe. This was accompanied by a wonderful feeling of peace and joy. It was almost as though I was floating! It is over twenty years now since this happened but it is as fresh as though it were yesterday. Completely out of nothing I found myself writing down some verses. People find it hard to believe but I honestly believe God just got hold of my hand and wrote the words down. The poem, as it turned out to be, was fourteen lines long and God just seemed to say it was to be called "The Gift of the Holy Spirit".

# THE GIFT OF THE HOLY SPIRIT

My life was so empty, lost, forlorn,
At times I wished I'd not been born.
For me no hope or future in life,
Just constant battles of meaningless strife.
Where is the purpose here for me?
Will someone help that I may see?
Then slowly things began to change;
At first it seemed a little strange,
A different feeling deep inside,
A peace and joy you cannot hide,
A whole new world so fresh and new
A deepening love so strong, so true.
A whole new power in Jesus' Name
My life will never be the same!

I came to realise that what had happened to me was that I had been "baptised or filled with the Holy Spirit." This was something that had been prayed for on my behalf before but this day became real. The Acts of the Apostles Chapter 19 Verses 1 to 6 speaks of this.

There is clearly a time for everything and God's timing is always perfect.

As regards the poetry it just began to flow from me. I was seeing with new eyes and as I experienced things, I wrote about it. By the end of March I had written at least thirty poems, and to this day this writing has never stopped. I would add that I cannot recall ever having written a poem of any sort before that wonderful day in February. I have now written over 2,500 and had a number of books published for me by Moorley's which has enabled me to share what I believe God has given me to a much wider audience.

Well over a year ago now someone asked if I had ever written any short stories. I replied that I had only ever written something for our own Church magazine. I thought nothing more of this but God had clearly opened a door through this person, though I didn't realise it at the time.

5

Early in 1999 I had joined the Association of Christian Writers only to find there were few members in the area where I live. I did however get in touch with someone in Wigan sending him one of my poetry books. A friend of his was producer of the Sunday Breakfast Programme on Greater Manchester Radio. It was suggested I get in touch with him by letter. This resulted in my going to the local studio one Sunday morning in November where I briefly shared my testimony and a few poems. When the programme was over this producer said they were looking for "Thought for the Day" type of material or short meaningful accounts on a religious theme. He happened to say that earlier in the programme someone had posed the question 'If Jesus walked the earth today would He have a Mobile Phone?' An incredible thought indeed, but as my wife and I travelled home I couldn't stop thinking about what had been said. Eventually I wrote a story around it. Further stories followed of a different nature as I began to reflect what scant detail there was regarding so many of the healings and miracles Jesus performed. Hence this book which is a combination of stories and poems linked together. I do hope you will be blessed by what you read.

**Andrew**

# IF JESUS WALKED THE EARTH TODAY WOULD HE HAVE A MOBILE PHONE?

What a question to ask you may say. You could easily dismiss the idea straightaway. It really is hard to imagine our Saviour using one isn't it? You could argue what on earth would He need something like that for, after all His communication lines to His Father were perfect? Three scriptures from John spring to mind to support this:- "I and the Father are one," (John 10 Verse 30), "The Father loves the Son and has placed everything in His hands," (John 3 Verse 35) and finally "I do nothing on my own but speak just what the Father has taught me," (John 8 Verse 28).

But what of His relationships with His disciples and with other people generally. Of course there was no problem on His side but one can only sense His frustration particularly in His dealings with those twelve men God had given to Him.

In Matthew particularly as in the other gospels we hear how He instructed them as to what they were to do and how to do it giving them authority to drive out evil spirits and to heal all diseases. There must have been much concern in His heart when He sent them out as to how they would go on. According to Mark's gospel, Jesus sent them out two by two. A wise move you may well say when you consider those sons of thunder!

A modern Jesus complete with mobile phone could make six calls every now and then to get a progress report! "Hello, is that you Andrew, how are you getting on, and Pete is he learning patience? I hope he is behaving himself and perhaps learning to listen to others more? That's good about all the sick being healed in that village, keep up the good work, I'll ring again next Saturday."

Jesus is thinking to himself I know which call I am going to leave till last. Well that's it, I've rung everyone now except James and John. Why did I put those two together? I suppose I couldn't separate them really being brothers and all that! Anything could happen with those two. The sick could become desperately ill – even die – if they have a bad day. I'll ring them up now – would you believe it they're engaged! You can imagine my relief when I finally get through and find everything is wonderful. God is using them mightily. O ye of little faith! All the worry was unnecessary but thank you Father for Your wisdom in delaying the introduction of mobile phones to the twentieth century. Well I have learnt a lesson in trusting You for everything. After all You gave me them in the first place and You know what You are doing.

I can relax now knowing (I should have known before) that everything is safe in Your hands but what's this You want me to do – send out the seventy two in the future! There'll be plenty of calls here – 36 a time. Where can I get batteries or new cards from in the desert? I'll run out of juice in no time. Yes Father You were very wise to leave it to the twentieth century – the mobile phone thing.

Father You know all things. You know how I would be tempted to give my mother a quick call when on that donkey on my way into Jerusalem, though it wouldn't have been that easy with all those branches in my way, never mind all the commotion, but just a quick ring to reassure her that all was well, even though I knew what was ahead of me. Come to think of it I would have looked silly with a phone stuck in my ear in the circumstances! I thank You again Father for Your wisdom!

On a more serious note there was that business with Lazarus – the brother of Mary and Martha. How inappropriate a call would have been there from Me just to say I was on my way etc. When the time came though it was hard to hear Mary say: "If You had been here, my brother would not have died." Delay in this case was not denial. There was a greater purpose in My delaying My arrival as the Father had ordained. New technology just could have intervened here to interfere with My Father's purposes, but then My Father knew and knows all things.

Modern aids can so easily get in the way of God's purposes for us don't you think, if we let them?

You see when it gets down to it if we are in the right relationship with our Heavenly Father we don't need any communication aids. We can trust Him for everything – can't we? Hasn't He brought us safely to the beginning of a new day? His track record is good – very good. He has never let us down. He will take care of things that we cannot do anything about. No, the problem is we have been taking too many incoming calls. We have allowed our line to get busy. When our relationship with Him is right, doesn't everything else just slot into place.

Perhaps tomorrow or even tonight we will spend a little less time on the phone and a little more time with Him. Then may be we will hear His voice silencing all others – that still small voice that brings joy to the longing heart.

## IS YOUR LINE BUSY?

"I haven't heard any call from God."
That is what so many say,
But then their line is always busy:
In truth where do you stand this day?

In a world of consuming darkness
It is Jesus everyone needs to see.
Isaiah heard the voice of the Lord
And responded "Here am I, send me!"

Go and tell the people:
The world cries out in its need
But many are rooted to the ground
Too preoccupied to hear or heed.

Where are you today I ask?
Are you in a position to hear the call?
Do worldly pursuits dominate your life
Or are you one who has joyfully surrendered all?

*"And we know that in all things God works for the good of those who love him, who have been called according to His purpose."*

# MORE THAN A CONQUEROR

The first weekend in December 1995 was a very exciting time for me in a totally different way. On Friday afternoon, 1$^{st}$ December, I went with Alison to Rochdale Infirmary to have a troublesome double tooth out. I was referred from my dentist in September, because the tooth in question had three roots! I arrived at the hospital around 2 00pm and by about 3 00pm I was lying down and the tooth was almost out. I had had a local injection so I could tell when it finally parted company with me. I kept hearing words of reassurance that I was doing well etc., as though it was some big thing. Soon after it was out I raised my head and felt somewhat dizzy, so I just relaxed. The next few minutes that followed all hell let loose as they say. I passed out, stopped breathing and the nursing staff were unable to feel a pulse. At the very moment that this happened, Alison was reading a Christian book in the waiting area; apparently she was really enjoying this book and was very engrossed in it when the Lord told her to put the book down and to pray! Needless to say, this is what she did, and then after she had prayed the 'CRASH' team started to dash into the Dental Department to try and revive me. I can't have been unconscious for long, and the next thing I remember is a nurse shouting my name as I came round. They transferred me to the Casualty Department where it was discovered that I had an irregular heartbeat and that they wanted to carry out more tests. I was subsequently transferred by ambulance to the Coronary Care Unit at Birch Hill Hospital, where I was immediately placed on a heart monitor. When I looked up at this monitor I could see the irregulation for myself, even though of myself I didn't feel too bad. On Saturday they tried to regulate the heartbeat by doing IVF treatment and were very surprised when this did not effect the necessary regulation. It was then decided that on Sunday they would attempt to regulate my heart by electric shock treatment. This procedure was carried out about 4.00pm and as I came out of the anaesthetic around 5.15pm the doctor whispered in my ear that it had worked! I recovered very quickly after this and was able to watch Songs of Praise and afterwards would you believe it 'Heartbeat'?

The wonderful thing in all of this is how the Lord has looked after me. I can only say that His ways are wonderful. There is every likelihood that I have had an irregular heart beat for some years and would explain why I have occasionally felt off and in recent times a little groggy. If I had continued to have an irregular heart beat the likelihood is that I would have had a heart attack or a stroke in a few years' time; as it is this has been spotted and corrected and I have to say that I feel really well now and am certainly more relaxed.

I shall certainly take things easier and not do anything silly as the irregular heart beat could come back at any time.

All of this glorifies God and reminds us all that our Heavenly Father is watching us and caring for us all the time and that He takes care of even the smallest details in our lives. Praise His Name.

# WE LIVE IN AN EVER CHANGING WORLD

How often have we heard this said?

We can look back over the last fifty years or so and see the advance in science and technology which has resulted in so many new inventions which have enriched our lives. The invention of the radio, television, telephone, computer etc., to name but a few, the wide range of household gadgets which make home life easier. Of course, with the introduction of all these things has come a degree of stress when they break down!

There was a time when a man or woman would enter an occupation and he/she would expect to remain in that job for the rest of their working life. Today most people can expect at least three career changes in their working lifetime.

All around us we see change and the constant pressure of the advertisers who assure us that our lives will be so much better if we purchase product A with a lifetime guarantee!

In sharp contrast to all this frantic activity stands our Lord and God who states, **"I the Lord do not change"** (Malachi 3 Verse 6). The Lord goes on to state **"Ever since the time of your forefathers you have turned away from my decrees and have not kept them. Return to Me and I will return to you."** How we need individually and collectively throughout this land to return to the Lord our God. Can you detect almost a cry of desperation in the Lord's voice even now?

We live in an age it seems which welcomes every new idea or invention on the basis that anything that has gone before can't be as good or is now obsolete. Perhaps the older generation of our day are not so convinced that everything new is an improvement on the old. Many older people are indeed frightened by the introduction of new ways of doing things and are very sceptical when changes are contemplated which affect their lives.

The only real security we have as Christians is that we serve an unchanging God. **"Jesus Christ is the same Yesterday, Today and Forever"** (Hebrews 13 Verse 8) is a wonderfully reassuring scripture in a world that is clearly out of control.

Many religious people are trying to convince us that somehow the God of the twenty first century will be different to the God of the twentieth century. Many religions are indeed founded on the non-acceptance of who Jesus really is. Jesus said, **"I and the Father are One"** (John 10 Verse 30). Jesus is God. Jesus came down to earth as God's Son and is now at the right-hand of the Father in glory. The error of so many religions is that they do not accept the Trinity. Father, Son and Holy Spirit – three but one and the same. The world would say three for the price of one! How wonderful that when a believer prays to God the minimum number present is four!! What an assurance there is in this fact alone.

We are most certainly to guard the Holy Fire and speak out against anything and anyone who questions what we know to be true. The truth is, that we as Christians live in an unchanging world because **"I the Lord do not change."** (Malachi again).

We read in James Chapter 1 Verse 16 and 17 **"Don't be deceived my dear brothers, every good and perfect gift is from above coming down from the Father of the heavenly lights who does not change like shifting shadows."** The Revised version of the bible puts it even better **"From the Father of lights with whom there is no variation or shadow due to change.".** No variation, no shadow – there is absolute certain security here.

When someone says to us despairingly "well we live in a changing world don't we?". we can agree but we can confidently state that we serve an **Unchanging God** – there lies our total security, and then we can share with that person the hope we have within us.

# GOD UNCHANGING
(James 1:16-18)

Do not be deceived dear brothers
By acts of fleshly love,
Every good and perfect gift
Comes down from Heaven above.

We, who in our own wisdom
Are unable to see His rearranging,
Know that He is the source of all light
The Eternal God, unchanging.

Through the Word of truth by His own will
He brought us into being,
Now we have been completely transformed
From darkness into seeing.

Amongst all His creatures then
We've been given pride of place,
Those who truly believe in God
Are indeed a blessed race.

# JESUS CHANGES WATER TO WINE

Weddings are wonderfully joyous occasions. At the time of Jesus' earthly ministry such celebrations seemed to go on forever.

We can well imagine that the whole village would be out celebrating this day. It really was an opportunity for old friends to meet together and share over food and wine.

The family would no doubt, like most be poor and they would hope there would be enough of everything. There did seem to be a lot of people there! Certainly more than they had expected.

Jesus was there along with the disciples and his mother who became aware that the wine had run out. All that was left was the dregs at the bottom of the wine jars. Recognising how acutely embarrassed the family would be Mary perhaps in desperation turned to Jesus. "They have no more wine," she said, implying 'do something.'

Mary was aware that her son was no ordinary man. Jesus Himself was beginning to understand if only in part what lay ahead for Him. His baptism was wonderful but His temptation had really shown Him what He was up against and He knew that there were many trials and tribulations ahead.

Expectations were high already as regards this carpenter's son, and Jesus knew if He were to meet the needs of this family supernaturally life would never be the same again. Perhaps our Lord had been weighing things up in His mind in the days following His desert encounters with Satan, and this would account for the nature of His reply.

"Dear woman, why do you involve me? My time has not yet come." Jesus said.

Not put off by His reply His mother said to the servants "Do whatever He tells you." Mary knew her son and that He would want to save the family embarrassment.

There were six stoneware water pots used for ritual washings by the Jews. Each held twenty to thirty gallons.

Jesus instructed the servants to "fill the jars with water" and they did so to the brim. "Now fill your pitchers and take them to the host." I wonder what those servants were thinking? Theirs was to do just as they were told of course, and they did. I am sure they realised that something had taken place but their expectation was perhaps not that of Jesus' mother!

The host of the banquet tasted the water that had now been turned into wine. He did not realise where it had come from or what had just happened but he was in for a very pleasant surprise. He exclaimed "Everybody I know begins with their finest wines and after the guests have had their fill then brings in the cheap stuff, but you have saved the best till now."

This was the first of many miraculous signs Jesus was to perform. The first glimpse of His glory you could say.

How this miracle shows us the true character of Jesus. Many would have chosen a completely different venue for our Lord to reveal His glory. Somewhere like the Imperial Palace in Rome where everyone would see and hear.

Jesus always responded to the needs presented to Him and so often in the future after healing a person He would tell them not to tell anyone. No the first miracle was a quiet affair and it was conducted in Cana, an obscure corner of Galilee.

The most important person of all saw the willingness in the heart of the Saviour to meet the needs of His people – God the Father. That was sufficient.

In this miracle we have a wonderful assurance that "the best is yet to come". We also have a sharp contrast between the ways of this world and the ways of the Kingdom. Whether we have only just become a Christian or have been one for fifty years we know assuredly that "the best is yet to come".

One day we will sit at the greatest banquet of all and we will drink of the choicest wine. I don't know about you but I can't wait!

******

# THE NEW WINE
(Based on John 2:1-11)


We joy in that first miracle
At Cana of Galilee
Yet the water of life
Still flows full and free.


In the world everyone brings out
The choicest wine at first
To satisfy the immediate needs
To quench the longing thirst.


The cheaper wine then follows
For the need has been satisfied
But the best is always to come
As we live for the Lamb who died.


Ahead for us the choicest fruits
For we know the finest wine
Will be served in the Kingdom
In His Presence Divine.

On a personal note my wife Alison and I had the privilege in June of 1998 of going to Israel with a party from our church. On the 11th June we were to go to Cana to visit a church which is built on the site of that first miracle.

We had been to Cana before 1998 and had visited this church and seen the wonderful history within its walls and some of the actual water jars which it is believed were of Jesus' day.

This visit was to be quite different for in the first place we were not allowed into the building by the main entrance but were directed to a side door which housed the newly renovated chapel.

Our initial disappointment was turned into joy as we walked into an actual wedding service, of what turned out to be two Americans, both of whom appeared to be widowed grandparents. We were handed an Order of Service and quietly made our way to some seats at the rear of the Church. The wedding had clearly been going on for a while and we soon found ourselves sharing in their joy.

We were in for a further surprise as the Minister within a few minutes of our arrival, invited all married couples present to renew their wedding vows. There was some sadness for those who had come to Israel leaving their husbands at home but great joy for Alison and I, particularly as we had been considering renewing our wedding vows for some time as when we were married in 1966 neither of us were Christians.

God knows the desire of our hearts. In John 16 Verse 30 as interpreted in "The Message" translation we read the disciples' conclusion regarding Jesus: "Now we know that You know everything – it all comes together in You."

On the 11th June 1998 in a church in Cana of Galilee everything came together for us in Christ. We joyfully, tearfully stood up and renewed our wedding vows. It is a day we will never forget.

# HE CAME BY NIGHT

In all the Gospel accounts we only hear of one member of the religious order of the day seeking out a private audience with the Saviour. Many must have been inwardly disturbed by Jesus. The things He did disturbed them but they were more disturbed by what He said.

The life of Nicodemus, a member of the Jewish ruling council, a man who was at the top of the religious ladder so to speak, was so arrested that finally he decided he must speak with this Jesus alone. It would have to be at night. He couldn't risk a day-time encounter.

After the scene when Jesus cleared the Temple of all the merchants it was the only option.

Spurred on by a stricken conscience this lonely figure, dressed in the least conspicuous clothing quietly slipped down the side streets. He hurried along fearful of being attacked let alone being noticed by anyone. He sighed with relief when he was in the open country.

How did he know where Jesus was? Perhaps he overheard the disciples talking or perhaps there was a small area where travellers tended to congregate.

With a sense of relief he sees one of the disciples and asks him can he see the Master. Jesus has found a quiet spot where He is praying to His Father. Those precious times were so meaningful as the days were hectic and long.

Jesus is made aware that there is a visitor. Perhaps He is surprised particularly when He sees who it is! Maybe their eyes had met before and the Master had seen the questioning need in this man's heart. It may well be that Nicodemus had been concerned for a long time at the way affairs were conducted both inside and outside the Temple. Jesus' words still rang in his ears, 'destroy this temple, and I will raise it again in three days.'. What audacity to say such a thing! As he pondered over those words he longed to know the deeper meaning behind them.

Nicodemus' first words to Jesus are really just something to steady his nerves, to calm himself down more than anything because I am sure he couldn't believe himself where he is standing now. "Rabbi, we know you are a teacher who has come from God. For no-one could perform the miraculous signs you are doing if God were not with him."

Jesus replied knowing exactly what this Pharisee needed: "I tell you the truth, no-one can see the Kingdom of God unless he is born again."

"How can a man be born when he is old?" Nicodemus asked. "Surely he cannot enter a second time into his mother's womb to be born!"

What an astounding answer from the Pharisee! We can see in this answer what a lifetime of study has done to him. Observing every jot and tittle of the law down the years has left him lifeless and with a mind bursting for answers. He recognises that here is a man – Jesus – who not only exudes life but also speaks the very words of life. In His presence his own deep-rooted inadequacies are highlighted all the more. His answer only reinforces what a problem intelligence is to so many people. It is quite ludicrous to come up with the question Nicodemus did.

Jesus then enlightens him more fully about the Kingdom of Heaven and the movement of the Spirit. Nicodemus is standing in the very presence of God for slowly he realises that this is the One of whom the Prophets spoke.

Like so many people he is but one step away but sadly again like so many he is cautious and careful. Could this be the Messiah? Deep down he knew the answer to that question but it is quite another thing in his position to openly declare it. His life really would have to change if he did that. He instead chose to be a secret believer, perhaps working in his own quiet way to try and influence those around him.

In contrast we who know the full truth are called to declare it openly. We truly are meant to speak of what we have seen and heard and accordingly go and make disciples of all nations baptising them in the name of the Father and of the Son and of the Holy Spirit and teaching them to obey everything He has commanded us to do.

This Great Commission as it is referred to has an even greater significance two thousand years on. We are truly called to be people of the Light. Perhaps we have languished in the darkness for too long!

Our friend Nicodemus came by night to the Light of the World. We once walked in the same darkness he did but now the Light has been revealed to us and what a marvellous Light it is! We really do have something wonderful to share with others.

## HE CAME BY NIGHT
(Based on John 3:1-21)

A member of the Jewish ruling council;
Men looked to him for what was right.
Nicodemus was however troubled and fearful
So he came to Jesus by night.

I must not be seen he thought to himself
As he walked down another side street.
His conscience however spurred him on
This Jesus I must meet!

There were many questions in his mind.
He so wanted to see
But his eyes alas were closed
For he asked "how can this be?"

"You must be born again"
Jesus' reply to him he saw as very odd
Then our Lord said "unless this happens
You cannot see the Kingdom of God."

Nicodemus came by night we know
And sadly he remained in the gloom.
"Surely a man cannot enter a second time
Into his mother's womb?"

The Pharisee's problem was his intelligence
And the fact he had much to lose.
So it was that the familiar path of caution
Was the one he was destined to choose.

He knew something was missing in his life
But what really could he do.
Maybe this was the Messiah speaking.
His words were so refreshingly new.

Nicodemus sadly waited to Jesus' death
Before he chose to honour His name.
The mixture of myrrh and aloes offered
Could in no way hide his shame.

We can all decide to wait till tomorrow
But tomorrow may be too late
Behold our Lord and Saviour sees us
He stands waiting by the open gate.

We have been languishing long in darkness
But He will meet us in our night,
He longs that we take a step of faith
And so enter His marvellous light.

# THE MEETING
(Based on John 4:1-26)

She wends her weary way in the heat of the day to the well. Jacob's Well was probably the only one in Sychar. It certainly was the nearest. The route was all too familiar for her, but these days she did it at a time when she would expect to meet no-one.

Her face bore the scars of five failed marriages. Her life was in tatters even though there was now a sixth man in her life. How long would this relationship last? This time she had chosen not to marry. Perhaps the wagging tongues of all the town dwellers had convinced her against marriage. Husband or no husband the emptiness of her life consumed her being and was reflected in the way she walked toward the well. Her only thought was to get there and back home as quickly as possible. It was a job that had to be done – the sooner the better.

She could see the well now. Her face dropped. She observed a figure sat by the well. As she drew closer she could see it was a man. There was some relief in that. He must be a stranger, which was a comfort to her but this was no ordinary person as she soon discovered.

Her mind went back to the time when men hadn't controlled her life. She used to go with the other women catching up with all the gossip on the way. It was almost like a picnic as they sat together round the well letting their hair down as they were free for at least a while from the male dominated society of their day. Then it was a trip at dusk making it so much easier to relax. Now she wishes she could turn the clock back and begin again or even run away and make a fresh start in a new town, but where would she go?

Her thoughts disappear as the stranger asks her for a drink. She can see he is a Jew. How can this be? Jews and Samaritans don't mix but she had heard Him clearly. More surprises are to come for the woman as Jesus talks of a different kind of water and proceeds to reveal His knowledge of her but without any condemnation. How uncomfortable she must feel as He exposes her past. She remarks that He must be a prophet.

She knows the Messiah will come one day and explain all things. You can't begin to imagine how surprised she is when Jesus says He is the Messiah! She doesn't know where to look. Can it be true? He speaks with authority.

There is something very wonderful and amazing here. God arranges for Jesus to go that particular way that day so she could meet with the only One who could help her and that at a time when she would expect to meet no-one. God could have sent Jesus to a whole crowd of people in any town or village but instead He sent Him to the one woman whose sheer desperation and emptiness of heart made her open to listening to the voice of the Master.

It was a different journey that day. It began with her feet to a well, but it became a deep journey of the heart. First she simply called Him a Jew then Sir, then a Prophet. Then she sees Him finally as the Messiah. The journey of discovery can be a very long one for so many people but for this troubled lady it all happened in a matter of a few hours.

With this revelation weariness leaves her body. The water jar is forgotten as she races back towards the town. Her legs are those of a young girl again. Such is the excitement in her voice that even those who normally ignore her are forced to turn in her direction and listen. Somehow they know where she has been. Something really special must have happened to her for her to leave her water jar at the well. What is she saying? Could this be the Messiah? There's only one way to find out. They go with her to where Jesus is. So it was they listened and believed for themselves who He was.

How often it is that the Lord uses the most unlikely people to spread His Kingdom. He sees and identifies the longing heart and then uses that heart to bring more hearts to Him.

The day began as any other day for this Samaritan woman. She awoke to the same old routine feeling worthless, a complete failure, with little or no future at all.  She ended it having met the only One who can change despair into hope and not only that she became a bringer of hope into the lives of others.

The story begins with Jesus on His way to Galilee from Judea having to go through Samaria.  He had to go to Sychar not to meet a big crowd but just one person.  This speaks of how our Lord wants to meet with each one of us individually in His own special way.  Nothing is too much trouble for Him.  He knows all about us and just wants to change us into His likeness.

Perhaps today will be a different day for us.  One we will never forget.  All we have to do is to make that journey to the well and rest awhile and just listen to what He has to say – just listen.

# TAKE TIME TO LISTEN

Dark clouds lie above me
There is silence in the skies.
My vision is so restricted now
It seems I have unseeing eyes.

Dullness now consumes my thinking;
My hearing has become impaired.
My feet have lost their spring:
I walk in the company of the scared.

My strength is all but gone,
I feel ever so weak.
No longer do I hear Your voice;
Have You ceased to speak?

My son I am with you
My tongue has never been still
My desire always is that you live
In accordance with My will.

There has been strength in My silence
That has occasioned your heart to fear.
You have looked for Me in vain;
Yet I have always been near.

You have not been taking the time
To listen intently for Me.
You have ears that do not hear;
And eyes that do not see.

Take time now to listen
Stand aside to hear My voice
Then I will cause the heavens to open
And your heart to rejoice.

# JESUS HEALS THE OFFICIAL'S SON
(Based on John 4:46-53)

Again Jesus visited Cana. This place probably had a special place in His heart as He remembered the previous time. Then it was a joyful occasion – a wedding but this time he was faced with great sadness.

A royal official almost certainly in Herod's employ desperately worried about his son's deteriorating health had decided he would make the twenty five mile journey from Capernaum to see if Jesus could help him. Being a wealthy man no expense would have been spared to make his boy well but there are things that high position with all the trappings cannot buy.

What a relief when he finally found Jesus and how surprised the people would be when they saw him begging before Jesus for his boy's life. This man was a Royal Official after all and maybe this act of itself surprised Jesus who always felt more at home with the ordinary people of His day.

This could account for what would appear to be a response that lacked compassion for in truth He rebuked the man. "Unless you people see miraculous signs and wonders," Jesus told him, "you will never believe." His statement was undoubtedly directed at all the people who had seen what he had done in Jerusalem, who were constantly wondering what He would do next. They needed to see beyond the healings and miracles to see for themselves the Kingdom of Heaven that our Saviour spoke so much about.

This story is in direct contrast to that of the Centurion who did not want to trouble the Master with a journey on behalf of his servant. "Just say the word, and my servant will be healed" were the words the Centurion used – and he was.

The royal official said, "Sir, come down before my child dies," believing that a personal visit was necessary for restoration to take place.

Jesus replied, "You may go. Your son will live."

The compassion of Jesus for His people and specially for children who always had a special place in His heart was not to be denied. As the official made his way home news came through that his boy was well and that the fever had left him at the exact time that Jesus had spoken.

This Royal Official perhaps inadvertently was being used to thwart God's true purposes. If Jesus had gone with him it would have been probably four days or more before He was back in Cana where He was clearly meant to be. It was, we are assured, some time later before Jesus went up to Jerusalem for a Feast. It would seem that a lengthy stay in Cana was what His Heavenly Father had planned.

When the official got home there would be joyful celebrations but the impact of Jesus' words must have hit home. All that needed to be said was "your son will live". Such was the power in those words alone that not only the official believed but all his household. A greater work was accomplished. A personal visit was not necessary. There was a double celebration in that home in Capernaum and even greater joy in heaven for we are assured when we read Luke's Gospel Chapter 15 Verse 7 that there is more rejoicing in heaven over one sinner who repents than over ninety-nine righteous persons who do not need to repent. A whole household was changed by just four words and maybe many more people's lives as those new believers shared what had just happened.

## "YOUR SON WILL LIVE"
(Based on John 4:46–53)

Jesus was always more at home
With the ordinary people of His day
So when a royal official came to Him
He had something much different to say.

Riches and positions of honour in this world
Are by so many sought
But they were no help to this official
Who was so clearly distraught.

Miraculous signs and wonders
Were what these people wanted to see
But this man was desperate
And came to Jesus on bended knee.

The royal official wanted Jesus
To come quickly before his child died.
There must have been amazement
In how the Saviour replied.

"You may go.  Your son will live."
What comfort to the broken-hearted!
So it was the official took Him
At His word and departed.

What thoughts must have been going on
In that official's questioning mind?
When he finally got to his home
What would he then find?

It wasn't long before the servants
Met their master with joy.
"He lives who was dying;
He lives, your precious boy!"

From within our mighty Saviour
There must have been a release of power
For the boy got better
When Jesus spoke at the seventh hour.

What joy at the official's home
We know the news was well received
For through this mighty miracle
All the household believed.

# THE HEALING AT THE POOL
## (Based on John 5:1-9)

We are assured there was a great number of people with various disabilities gathered round this pool which was near the Sheep Gate. This pool at Bethesda represented the only chance of a changed life for so many who had been sick for years. One can only picture the pain, distress and continued disappointment of so many who were either brought there at the beginning of the day by friends or relatives or whose lives were such that Bethesda had become their home.

The disappointment would only intensify for so many when the pool was stirred. It was believed that an angel of the Lord came down from time to time to stir up the waters but only the first one in would be cured of whatever disease they had. The time between these stirrings or movings would represent a ray of hope to so many but increasingly the disappointments would cast a lengthening shadow on the whole area. For many all hope seemed to have gone and any change in their life could represent a threat or cause fear in the heart.

One man, who we know nothing about, had been an invalid for thirty eight years and presumably had spent much of it at Bethesda. What was this man's level of expectancy? We can only imagine it had reached an all time low.

If he had seen Jesus I am sure he would have cried out loud above the noise of the area but it was Jesus who first saw him stretched out by the pool where He learned how long he had been in this condition.

It wasn't that long before when Jesus' encounter with one woman at a well caused the transformation of the whole town of Sychar. This woman's words "Come see a man who told me everything I ever did" began the change and many people became believers as a result.

How this contrasts with the scene at Bethesda. Here only one man's life was to change and that when Jesus asked this invalid a very purposeful question. "Do you want to get well?"
How could Jesus looking at the man ask a question like that?

Of course he did, we hasten to reply. The reality is however that many people down the years have got used to a disabled state. They have come to love all the care and attention lavished on them. In this man's case it was probably not like that at all but Jesus was really saying to him "do you really want your life to change?" So many have got comfortable with things the way they are, however unpalatable that may be to the casual observer.

One can sense more than a hint of desperation in his reply: "Sir, when the water is stirred, I don't have anybody to help me into the pool. By the time I get there someone else is already in." Jesus then said to him. "Get up! Pick up your mat and walk." At once the man was cured; he picked up his mat and walked.

However discreetly Jesus spoke with the man there must have been a number of people who saw what happened. It wasn't long before the man was told off by the Jews for breaking Sabbath rules, by carrying his mat, but surely nothing could take his joy away! Thirty eight years of anguish and pain were removed in seconds. He had spent a good part of his life round that pool but now there was no need to go anywhere near it again except perhaps to give thanks to God for his healing as later he would come to realise who had spoken to him that day.

We continue to marvel at the mysterious ways of our Heavenly Father who sees and knows everything. Jesus may well have asked the Father for the power to heal everyone there. That would be totally consistent with His compassionate nature.

There are so many questions we could ask but clearly it was the Father's will that day to change the life of one man only and accordingly Jesus was sent to do just that. This was to be followed later by Jesus being directed to him at the Temple. With words that carried with them a very strong warning "See, you are well again, stop sinning or something worse may happen to you." It could well be that the man was not ready to hear such a strong warning earlier in the day. There was a greater responsibility now for this man to take on board. He had to begin to live a new kind of life. Jesus had no doubt been prompted by His Father to give this man his mobility back because there were greater purposes ahead for him.

The healing of this man that day was surely only a part of this. We know that when our heavenly Father causes a change to take place in us whether large or small it is a prelude to a greater movement still.
Jesus said "My food is to do the will of Him who sent me." Perhaps we can come to full agreement with Jesus when He said "Not My will be done but Yours." May we be in a position to continuously embrace all that that means for we have a God who wants to do more in and through us than we can ever imagine.

Now to Him who is able to do exceedingly abundantly above all that we ask or think, according to the power that works in use, to Him be glory in the church by Christ Jesus to all generations forever and ever. Amen. (Ephesians 3 Verses 20 & 21).

# THE HEALING AT THE POOL
### (Based on John 5:5-9)

He had no one to help him
When the water was stirred.
Until that precious moment
His cries remained unheard.

In terror and in pain,
An invalid for thirty eight years
But there came that day a man
Who took away all his fears.

Jesus, the Great Healer,
The supplier of every need
Asked "do you want to get well?"
A simple question indeed.

"Every time I try to get in the pool
Someone else goes down ahead of me."
His plight could not have gone unnoticed
But no one chose to see.

His only desire was to reach the pool
To end his years of hell
But there was so much more contained
In Jesus' words: "Do you want to get well?"

He never made it to the pool that day
We are reliably assured.
"Pick up your mat and walk."
At once the man was cured.

How easy it is to limit God's power
When looking at our own situation.
In his dealings with us, our Lord always exceeds
Our highest expectation.

# A VERY SPECIAL DAY

The story of the feeding of the five thousand is the only miracle recorded in all four gospels and only in John's account is a boy specifically mentioned.

For this small Galilean boy it was to be a very special day. We don't know anything about him except that he came from a poor family – the lunch he carried of coarse ground barley bread along with the fish indicated that.

The young boy must have heard of this Jesus and the wonderful miracles He had been doing and was determined to see for himself and to keep up with the crowd. He could not imagine that he himself would be used in one of these miracles!

His little legs must have been tired and we can assume that like all boys of his age after a long day he was getting very hungry and would welcome a sit down.

Suddenly one of the disciples came towards him having noticed his lunch box. This disciple Andrew spoke up and Jesus took notice. What followed was amazing! Two miracles were to take place of a totally different nature. The first miracle was that one very hungry boy parted company with his food! Maybe he looked into the eyes of Jesus and his questioning ceased and simultaneously he found his hands opening wide.

The surrender of that food precipitated a great miracle – one of the greatest ones of the Bible. Jesus had a habit of taking the very simple and ordinary and doing something extraordinary. We remember how God used a young shepherd boy with a slingshot to slay a giant!

We learn from this that all we really need to do is to place into God's Hands what we have – just like the little boy – so He can use it. Thousands of people were nourished in every way because one little boy said yes in his heart. He could so easily have refused to part with his lunch and run away from the scene but he didn't. He stayed and his life was blessed along with the lives of so many others! Maybe this was the beginning of a new life for him and as he came to fully understand what had happened so he became a true follower of Jesus.

One thing this small boy has left with us is the eternal message of the beauty and joy of self-surrender and an ever present reminder that whatever we place into His hands He will not only bless it but cause it to multiply!

Jesus made the people sit down. Perhaps we need to just sit down and look afresh at this wonderful story and where we are in our daily lives.

How easy it is to hold back when we should just let go. We allow all sorts of things to detract us or deflect us from what God means to achieve in and through us.

Two thousand years ago one little boy let go of a lunch box and a huge crowd was fed. What a story he had to tell when he got home! When the time comes for us to go home may we truly be able to offer to God empty hands.

The surrender of a child and the compassion of a Saviour were all that were needed that day. We can so easily look at what little we have and consider it to be nothing but if we put the little we have into God's Hands then anything can happen! Ask the little boy, he will tell you.

One day in Heaven we may just meet up with him and he will be able to tell us the full story of that very special day when he and so many others tasted the bread that came down from Heaven. Something I am sure for us all to look forward to!

# OUR RESOURCES
(Based on John 6:9)

"How far will they go
Among so many?
The Lord can use your pounds
And He can use a penny.

Bring to Him what you have
Whether large or small.
Just bring your whole self;
Give to Him your all.

How easy it is to withhold
Or simply fritter away
That which we have kept
For a rainy day.

It was the loaves and fish
The gift of that small boy
That caused Heaven to come down
Bringing such joy.

Offer to Jesus your resources now.
Don't let another day go by,
Let Him take them in His arms
Then watch them multiply.

# THE WOMAN CAUGHT IN ADULTERY

We know nothing of this woman's past. It would seem that she earned her living by giving service to men. How did all this begin? Could it be traced to an unhappy childhood – a childhood where she was deprived of real love? In her search for love had she reluctantly become a prostitute? There seemed no way out of her unhappy life but a recent client had said to her that she had a friend. The friend of sinners – this Jesus – was in town.

How could she meet with Him? Such was the opposition to her in her immediate locality that she dare not set foot out of her door during daytime hours. She got young boys to do errands for her to provide the essentials she needed. This added to her unpopularity, as caring parents did not want their children near her house.

Just the thought that there was someone in town who could possibly help her get out of her present situation caused her spirit to lift. She wanted an end to the way she lived. It had been all right at first but the novelty had soon worn off. She was so well known and for all the wrong reasons. She needed a new start. Was it possible for someone like her?

People were always peeping and nosing around her windowsill. No doubt the Teachers of the Law and the Pharisees were under pressure to do something about her.

Now this troublesome Teacher was here as well. He was definitely queering their patch and humiliating them, as they saw it, in front of the very people they were meant to instruct and guide. Was this an opportunity to kill two birds with one stone – to get rid of this woman and to discredit this Jesus?

Two witnesses would be needed. It wouldn't be too hard to get two men to eavesdrop on her home and forcibly bring her caught in the act to the Temple courts. At the same time allowing her lover to slip away perhaps through a window, unnoticed.

The Pharisees and Teachers of the Law must have thought at last we have trapped Him. They made her stand before the group of people listening to His teaching and spoke to Jesus: "Teacher, this woman was caught in the act of adultery. In the law Moses commanded us to stone such women. Now what do you say?"

There was no hurried reply from the Saviour. The Pharisees and Teachers of the Law posed no threat to our Lord who was always in perfect relationship with His Father. How anxiously they must have waited for His reply but Jesus just bent down and started to write on the ground with His finger. How that must have infuriated them!

Then after what seemed an eternity He straightened up and said to them: "If any one of you is without sin, let him be the first to throw a stone at her." Then He carried on writing on the ground which can only have left them gobsmacked.

The impact of His words was immediate as one by one the accusers left the scene. Soon there was just the woman amazed at what had occurred.

Jesus straightened up again and asked her: "Woman, where are they? Has no-one condemned you?"

"No-one Sir," she said.

"Then neither do I condemn you," Jesus declared, "Go now and leave your life of sin."

We can be sure that she did leave her life of sin and maybe she really was young enough to start again. She must have felt wonderfully loved by the Saviour and very much challenged about the way she had lived.

Maybe she moved away from her surroundings and began a new life. Maybe also she found a man to share that new life with and the blessing of having her own family.

It all began when one man stood up for her when all the world was against her. Her days of condemnation were over for there is no condemnation for those in Christ Jesus.

A few years hence you can just picture her sat with a child on each knee re-telling the day when Jesus changed the whole direction of her life. He is still doing the same thing today, for those who recognise the need for change.

# THE WOMAN CAUGHT IN ADULTERY
(John 8:1-11)

All the people gathered round Him
They listened as He taught.
Then a woman caught in adultery
Was by the Pharisees brought.

"Caught in the act, she should be stoned to death,
Jesus what do you say?"
The Teachers of the Law and the Pharisees
Were trying to trap Him in some way.

They desired to accuse Him
As they gathered around
But He just bent over and wrote
With His finger on the ground.

As they stood there asking Him questions,
He slowly raised His head.
Straightening Himself up.
These words to them He said.

"Whichever one of you has committed no sin
May throw the first stone."
It wasn't long before Jesus was left
With the woman alone!

For on hearing His words
The bold became the faint-hearted.
One by one; the older ones first
They very soon departed.

"Is there no one left to condemn you?"
"No-one Sir," she said.
"Where have they gone,
It would seem they've all fled.

I do not condemn you either.
Be honoured now before all men.
Go forward in My name
Do not sin again!"

# IF YOU ARE WILLING, YOU CAN
# MAKE ME CLEAN
(Based on Mark 1:40-45)

This man was covered with leprosy, which begins with little specks on the eyelids, and on the palms of the hand. It then spreads over the entire body not only attacking the outside but the inside as well.

The nature of the disease of which there was no cure forced this man to live outside the walls of the city in a leper colony.

If he was a family man what pain for him and those he loved. Gradually he would lose his friends for they would increasingly become scared for themselves; such was the magnitude of the illness. His contact with his wife and children would still be maintained but gradually he would see less of them as his condition deteriorated.

How he longed to embrace his wife and children as he had done in the past but alas no more. There were lips that could not be kissed and hands that could not be touched. His family would be unaware how little feeling he had in his limbs.

How difficult it must be for them to just keep coming with their provisions every time seeing a slight deterioration in his condition. Perhaps by now the children had stopped coming and the visits by his wife and mother had become less frequent. Every time they came they would go away heartbroken. Perhaps they were thinking how long must he go on suffering.

The attitude of the ordinary people towards lepers was bad enough but it was nothing compared to that of the rabbis. On top of the physical stigma they believed it to be a direct moral blow by God on the backs of the sinful with all that that implied. Leprosy for them was a visual symbol of moral decay. What a dreadful presumption and how this contrasted with the compassionate way Jesus looked upon those inflicted so.

Word somehow got through to this leper that Jesus was in town. He would try and get near Him and beg for help. Desperation overtook him as he saw the crowds in front of him. He was determined. He would force his way into the presence of Jesus and just fall on his knees before Him. If anyone could help him this man could.

Suddenly he was there in front of the Master, "If You are willing, You can make me clean." The words just tumbled out of his broken, disfigured face.

Jesus then filled with compassion reached out His hand and touched the man. "I am willing," He said, "Be clean!" Immediately the leprosy left him and he was cured.

Jesus then instructed him to tell no one but go directly to the priest and offer the sacrifices that Moses commanded for cleansing, as a testimony to them.

The man was perhaps so excited and overwhelmed with what had happened that there was only one thought in his head – his family. There was so much lost time to be made up! Would his children even recognise their dad? What a surprise was in store for his family. How wonderful to have their father back from the very jaws of death. We can only imagine their joy.

Perhaps he did find time to show himself to the Priest. I am sure he would do, to honour what the Lord said, but surely we can all forgive him for not doing things in quite the right order.

Jesus Himself was sentenced to a few days when He had to be "outside the town" in "lonely places" because of the man's disobedience. There were to be many lepers who would be rescued from such "lonely places" in the coming weeks and months ahead.

The wonderful news for all of us is that Jesus wants to fill the emptiness in our lives. He wants to take us from those "lonely, outside places" and truly bring us "home" to live with Him, not just for a few days but forever.

# A MAN WITH LEPROSY
## (Mark 1:40-45)

Large crowds followed Jesus
As He came down the mountainside.
There He was greeted by a leper
As others sought to run and hide.

Leprosy was so very contagious,
Everyone near was ill at ease,
When this man came to Jesus
And fell down at His knees.

Desperation was in his every movement.
In the falling he would be seen.
Then the cry "Lord, if You are willing
You can make me clean."

Jesus reached out His hand
And touched the troubled, weary soul.
"I am willing" He said, "Be clean."
The leprosy left him, immediately he was whole.

Jesus then warned him to say nothing
As He sent him away.
He was to go and show himself
To the priest without further delay.

But the man couldn't keep it to himself
How difficult it is for you and me
To keep silent when we want to tell the world
That Jesus has set us free!

# AN ENCOUNTER WITH A GREEK WOMAN

Jesus made a brief visit to the region of Tyre and Sidon. There was purpose in this as there was with everything the Saviour did. The Son of Man, who frequently had nowhere to lay His head withdrew to this area presumably because He had this house to go to for rest. The journey had been long. An opportunity to recharge the batteries we would say.

Jesus couldn't escape notice. He thought no one had seen Him enter the house but one very determined woman must have known He was making His way there. Her daughter was possessed by an evil spirit. How she had suffered seeing her beloved daughter in such a disturbed state.

She cried out "Lord, Son of David, have mercy on me! My daughter is suffering terribly from demon possession." Her cry though clearly heard goes unnoticed it seems. We can only assume that Jesus was as usual in direct communication with His Father for His initial reply is not what we might have expected. "I was sent only to the lost sheep of Israel." Clearly that was the Saviour's calling but could He refuse this desperate woman?

The woman had come so far and was not going to give up now. She came and knelt before Him. "Lord, help me," she said.

Jesus' reply is staggering but it seems the woman was ready for it even before He spoke. An amazing dialogue took place.

Jesus said, "It's not right to take bread out of children's mouths and throw it to the dogs."

She quickly replied: "But even the dogs eat the crumbs that fall from their master's table."

I am sure Jesus was amazed by this reply and the faith of the woman. Our Lord was frequently disappointed by the faith of those who He was sent to but mightily encouraged by the faith of non-Jews. How encouraged He was earlier by the faith of the centurion.

In astonishment He said then to those following Him: "I tell you the truth, I have not found anyone in Israel with such great faith." (Matthew 8 Verse 10). All the centurion needed was 'a word' from the Saviour. His servant was healed instantly.

Jesus answered the woman now: "Woman you have great faith! Your request is granted." Just like the servant earlier her daughter was healed at that very hour.

There is certainty with the Saviour. What He says He will do. The Greek woman may have faced a long journey home but it was not a wearisome journey, it was a walk of joyful faith. Every step taking her nearer home – to a new home and to a new daughter. The words of the Saviour ringing in her ears. At times she must have broken into a run. Suddenly she was a young girl again. That is what an encounter with the Saviour does!

What a lesson of faith and perseverance this is for us. If we really believe and trust in Jesus we can confidently expect that when we return home. Whatever the problem was it will be gone, for is He not the same yesterday, today and forever? (Hebrews 13 Verse 8)

# THE FAITH OF THE GREEK WOMAN
(Based on Matthew 15:21-28 and Mark 7:24-30)

Jesus continued on His travels
Now He came to the region of Tyre.
There He was to fulfil
A woman's innermost desire.

She cried out 'Lord' then fell at His feet;
She desperately wanted to be heard.
Her daughter demon-possessed was suffering
But Jesus did not answer a word!

This lady loved her daughter so very much.
What pain she must have gone through!
Then to hear Jesus saying the lost sheep of Israel
Are those who I was sent to.

Was she excluded? – she wasn't for giving up.
The disciples wanted her out of their sight
"Lord help me," she tearfully cried out
From the depth of her darkest night.

She was ready to eat the crumbs
That fell from the children's table.
Anything if only her precious daughter
Could again be fit and able.

She was happy to be counted with the dogs
This determined and caring Greek,
Jesus' cause may have been to His own
But her perseverance prompted Him to speak.

Our Lord was taken aback by her reply;
From Him was now released the power.
"Woman of faith your request is granted"
Her daughter was healed that very hour!

What a lesson in perseverance for us all.
We must keep faith and move on.
The joy of this woman will be ours
When we return home and find the problem gone.

# THE HEALING OF A DEAF AND MUTE MAN

Jesus now left the region of Tyre and went through Sidon back to Galilee Lake and over to the district of the Ten Towns.

So often it seems Jesus was sent by His Father quite long distances just to meet the needs of one person. This only serves to show how important each one of us is to God the Father. Zeal for His Father's house consumed Jesus so there was no hesitation on His part when called to action. Perhaps the disciples didn't always share Jesus' enthusiasm! The tireless pursuit of lost souls and the physical needs of people spurred our Lord on in a way that the disciples could only partially comprehend.

Now a man is brought to Jesus who can neither hear nor speak. The people with him begged Jesus to place His hand on their friend. Everyone there was no doubt expecting Jesus to act immediately but our Lord took him aside, away from the crowd. Perhaps our Saviour had some faith-building words to impart to the man. Later on our Lord was to do a similar thing when at Bethsaida. There He took a blind man outside the village to restore his sight.

Away from the crowd, Jesus put His fingers into the man's ears. Then He spat and touched the man's tongue. Jesus looked up to Heaven and with a deep sigh said to him "Ephphatha" (which means "Be opened"). At this, the man's ears were opened, his tongue was loosened and he began to speak plainly.

Jesus urged those who were aware of what had happened to keep it quiet. How hard it is to remain silent when such a wonderful healing has just taken place! The people were overwhelmed with amazement and said, "He has done everything well. He even makes the deaf hear and the mute speak."

This man was now able to freely communicate with his friends and not only that he could hear everything they said. Perhaps he could echo David's words: "But I trust in you, O Lord; I say, Your are my God. My times are in Your hands." (Psalm 31 verses 14 and 15)

Perhaps he also could say: "You have done everything well, in your time."

The man may have waited many months just to see Jesus and would expect just a few words from our Saviour. After all His time was precious and He had so many places to go to and people to see.

The amazing thing is that our Lord was probably sent by His Father to that area for the healing of just this one man. Even then Jesus took him on one side and spent further time with him before freeing him of his infirmities.

How this speaks to us. We are all special to our Heavenly Father and how He longs to spend time with each one of us. May His longing become our longing.

# HE HAS DONE EVERYTHING WELL
(Based on Mark 7:31-37)

Jesus had come a long way
But it wasn't just an ordinary walk.
He was directed by His Father to a man
Who was deaf and could hardly talk.

The man who so longed for healing
Was not to be denied
But first away from the crowd
He was to be taken to one side.

Jesus put His fingers in the man's ears
Then spat and touched the man's tongue
It wouldn't be long now before
His heart would burst into song.

Jesus looked up to Heaven in prayer
And groaned mightily as if in pain.
"Be opened," He said and it happened.
The man's hearing was clear, his speech plain.

The things that had just occurred
No one was to tell
But the amazed people could only say
"He has done everything well."

Jesus always comes to those
Who confess that they are weak.
He it is who makes the deaf hear
And the mute speak.

Father we come to You today.
It's Your presence we desire.
We long for Your Kingdom to come
Please rekindle the dying fire.

# A BLIND MAN HEALED AT BETHSAIDA

Again Jesus had fed thousands of people miraculously. He now crossed the Lake and came to Bethsaida where a remarkable and very personal healing was to take place.

A man who was blind was brought to Jesus by some people who begged that our Lord would touch him. So often Jesus healed people brought to Him in an instant with just a few meaningful words spoken to their hearts. On this occasion not a word was said. Jesus just took the blind man by the hand and led him outside the village.

I wonder what those responsible for him were thinking? Where is He taking him? You can almost hear their questioning hearts. Then they would reason that this Jesus knew what He was doing. The fact that their friend was in good hands was some consolation. Nevertheless they felt very responsible for him.

Jesus spat on the man's eyes, put His hands on him and then asked, "Do you see anything?" Perhaps Jesus had been speaking to him on their walk to the outskirts of the village in order to build up his faith. This could well have been necessary, in this case, as a prerequisite to a complete healing. Jesus always did and does deal with each one of us in an individual way recognising that we are all made different.

The man looked up and said: "I see people; they look like trees walking around." Perhaps there was still a degree of unbelief in the man that prevented the full release of God's healing powers. Maybe Jesus saw faith rising up within him so once more He put His hands on the man's eyes. Then they were opened, his sight was restored, and he saw everything clearly.

We don't know how long the man had been blind but he saw clearly not only all that was around him but the face of the man who had wonderfully restored his sight. He was looking into the very face of God! How excited and how thankful he must have been.

How he now wanted to be reunited with his friends who had cared enough to bring him to Jesus, but Jesus sent him home saying: "Don't go and tell anyone in the village."

I wonder if he did keep Jesus' wishes. Perhaps he fully intended to at the outset but people would soon notice that he was different by looking at his face and of course would soon realise that he could now see.

How hard it is to keep something like this to yourself. His friends would perhaps be the first to be told. They wouldn't find it easy to keep it to themselves either. It wasn't every day that someone was miraculously healed though these occurrences were becoming more common.

Speaking as someone who himself has been wonderfully healed by the Saviour from a back injury it is almost impossible to keep quiet! No restrictions were imposed on me and how I rejoice to tell people what God has done. I only want to bring glory and honour to the name of Jesus.

I am sure that man two thousand years ago felt just the same.

******

# A BLIND MAN HEALED AT BETHSAIDA
(Based on Mark 8:22-26)

Jesus and the disciples arrived
At Bethsaida in Galilee.
There some people brought to Jesus
A man who couldn't see.

The people must have loved
This man very much
So they begged Jesus to
Give him a healing touch.

Jesus for some reason
Did not heal him there and then
But proceeded to take him away
From the eyes of curious men.

Jesus led him out of the village
Taking him by the hand
The man must have thought
He was going to a foreign land.

From what was familiar to him
He was taken away
Jesus was to restore him
But there was to be a delay.

When Jesus spat on the man's eyes
He must have wondered what was happening
Then our Lord put His hands on him
And asked: "Do you see anything?"

The man then looked up
Clearly he was ill at ease
When he said: "I see men
They look like walking trees."

Jesus laid hands on his eyes again.
Soon the man realised he had perfect sight.
His eyes were completely restored.
Everything was now clear and bright.

Jesus then sent him on home
Saying into the village you must not go
But when something like this happens to you
You want to tell everyone you know.

When in truth everyone can tell
That you are simply not the same
How you want to just bring
Glory and honour to Jesus' name!

# THE RICH YOUNG RULER

He was a young man who had everything – everything, that is, that money could buy. There was however something missing in his life. As we all know there are some things money can't buy.

A growing sense of inner dissatisfaction compelled this young man to look for Jesus that day. He had heard so much about His wonderful teaching and the amazing things He had done. He would go and see for himself.

What were the thoughts going through his mind as he made his way towards the crowds? Would he even get to speak to Jesus? He convinced himself he would and also that his question would be answered in a satisfactory way. As he got closer to where Jesus was perhaps his confidence began to ebb away, for by the time he reached the Teacher all he could do was fall on his knees before him.

"What must I do to inherit eternal life?" The question was anxiously arrowed in Jesus' direction. There must have been some desperation in his voice but it couldn't have been born out of a desire for real change to take place in his own life. His attitude was perhaps more of a person who had it all and was just looking for the final piece in the jigsaw. It was Jesus who held that final piece but it required surrender of all the other pieces for the picture to be completed. Like so many before and since he wasn't prepared for what Jesus had to say.

"Go, sell everything you have and give to the poor and you will have treasure in heaven. Then come and follow me."

Jesus' words must have hit him like a dagger piercing his heart. He wasn't expecting a reply like that! There was a price to pay for that missing piece of the jigsaw – a high price! For all of us there is something in the way that has to go before we can receive that "treasure in heaven."

Sadly the young man went away. His wealth was too much of an obstacle. It was indeed a hard test for him, and I am sure Jesus' heart went out to him as He saw the figure slowly disappear from sight.

How many times have we walked away if not physically but in our hearts when our Lord has been prompting us to a certain course of action. We may not be wealthy as the young man undoubtedly was but we do have something that no one can put a price on and something that no one can take away from us.

We have received a priceless treasure. Shouldn't we guard with our lives what has been entrusted to our care?

## *"ONE THING YOU LACK"*

# THE LORDSHIP OF JESUS CHRIST
(Based on Mark 10:21)

To the rich young man
"One thing you lack," He said.
"What is that thing with you
That is not yet dead?

What are you hanging on to?
That is causing the delay
To the fulfilment of His purposes
For you this day?"

You say: "Look I've got this and that in life."
Rather like someone holding cards in their hands.
"I just want to add the Lord Jesus Christ,
I know He hears and He understands."

You say: "With You Lord all will be well,
I will have a complete hand."
But you can never say that to Jesus Christ,
As though you've got everything planned.

He is not something to be added on
All else has to be laid aside
If you are truly to have
A place by His side.

Jesus can only come as Lord
If all the cards are laid down.
There is no easy route for anyone
Who desires to wear His crown.

# THE WIDOW'S MITE

What a difficult few days Jesus had faced. As He entered Jerusalem on that colt there was great joy in the hearts of the people but an equal measure of sadness in His. He knew at least in part what was ahead.

In the Temple Courts, after He turned over the tables of the money changers and the benches of those selling doves, He was faced with a barrage of questions from the Pharisees and Teachers of the Law who carefully put them together with the sole purpose of trying to trap Jesus. Of course our Lord was aware of this.

Jesus then remarked how the Teachers of the Law paraded themselves around for all to see in the market places and how wherever they went they sought out the best seats. This they did and at the same time they exploited people like widows who were weak and helpless.

After all the questioning our Lord must have been exhausted so He sought a place to rest yet where He could observe what was going on in the Temple area. He found a quiet place on a bench opposite the Treasury.

It was Passover so contributors were many and gifts would accordingly be at a seasonal high. Jesus saw many rich people throw large amounts in the coffers but His eyes were drawn to another figure who stood patiently in line ready to offer what little she had. Two copper coins probably representing the smallest offering the Temple allowed and certainly all this poor widow had to live on, were finally given.

No-one in the Temple area heard the sound of those coins as she dropped them in the coffers but in Heaven there was rejoicing.

It is remarkable that a very tired Jesus should notice this widow standing there when nobody else so much as looks. He waves His disciples over. It is important that they see this widow's great sacrifice in the light of the even greater sacrifice that is shortly to come.

Jesus said, "I tell you the truth, this poor widow has put more into the Treasury than all the others.  They all gave out of their wealth;  but she, out of her poverty, put in everything – all she had to live on." You can almost sense the enthusiasm in His voice.

This widow had every excuse or reason not to do what she did.  So much was given at Passover that she could excuse herself saying her gift was not needed.  What difference would her measly offering make and she could also so easily look at the way money was spent by, in most cases, corrupt religious leaders.

All these thoughts if they did exist in her mind were set aside.  She was giving to God and His work.  It was not for her to get into the area of politics.  She gave from a full and generous heart faithfully to God and she knew that in doing that God would support her.

How refreshing it must have been for our Saviour after all that had gone before to see that widow standing in line ready to give her all.

How easy it is for us to give as the others there did – what we will never really miss.  In a few days' time Jesus was to give His all that we might live.  Shouldn't we who have received so much from His hands be ready to stand in line behind the widow ready to give our all for His cause?

# SHE GAVE ALL
## (Based on Mark 12:41-44)

Jesus sat down opposite the temple treasury.
He chose for Himself a quiet place
But one where He could see the offerings made:
It was then He noticed a special face.

She stood out among the rich people.
She who could barely afford to live.
With her two copper coins she waited patiently
Until it was her time to give.

Nobody seemed to notice her
Except the most important One of all.
He noticed, He always does
What others consider to be small.

Jesus called over His disciples
This time they needed to be very near
So many things they had not grasped before
But now they really needed to hear.

There must have been great joy
And excitement in the Master's voice
On seeing the widow offering her coins
Inwardly His heart could only rejoice.

Jesus indeed joyfully recognised
The extent of the widow's offering
She gave out of her poverty
Not holding back a thing.

In the day when all things are remembered
There will still be cause for great delight
For that day when Jesus noticed
The widow giving her mite.

# THE WIDOW AT NAIN
## (Based on Luke 7:11-17)

Nain, overlooking the valley of Jezreel, was normally a quiet town but this day was going to be very different.

Never had it seen so many people invading its serenity. There were two contrasting crowds that day – one that followed Jesus joyfully sharing the wonderful things they had seen and heard and in stark contrast another crowd consumed with sadness – a funeral procession.

All the town was out to share this widow's distress. It didn't seem long ago when she had buried her husband and now her only son! It had been so sudden – one minute he was with her, the next he was no more. Burials were almost immediate in these hot climates. She couldn't take in what was happening to her and what of the future? There didn't seem to be one.

As so often is the case when all seems lost and the future seems hopeless we find Jesus in our midst. The widow's tear-filled eyes could only partially make out the figure in front of her. It is quite likely that she didn't even know who Jesus was.

Perhaps she felt the compassion in His heart. It clearly went out to her as He said "Don't cry." We are not told how she reacted to these seemingly insensitive words. After all she had every reason to cry. What had she to live for now?

What followed was truly amazing! In the first place Jesus touched the coffin which would have rendered Him unclean in the eyes of rabbinic law. But this was not a time for protocol.

Eight words then were spoken by the Saviour which must have caused a great fear to come upon the crowd. "Young man, I say to you get up." Immediately he did so. How could he refuse? He began to talk but we are not told what he said but surely the first word he spoke was "Mother."

Jesus gave him back to her – what a moment! She hadn't asked for anything but received everything. An incredible display of the Saviour's power and compassion was witnessed by the now two united crowds of people.

God had indeed come to His people. How quickly the news would spread everywhere about Jesus. It would be a long time before normality would return to that usually quiet town. After all there was a constant reminder of God's amazing love for His people whenever that young man was seen.

We all have a story to tell of what Jesus has done and continues to do for us. May we go out today mightily encouraged by this wonderful account, to tell people of the tremendous difference Jesus can make in your life.

# THE WIDOW AT NAIN
(Based on Luke 7:11-17)

The crowds were all around her
As she stood in deepest pain
A woman at her only son's funeral
How tragic for this widow at Nain.

Great sadness filled the village
Why did this young man have to die?
The Lord saw her and His heart went out to her
He lovingly said, "Don't cry."

The crowd looked on in utter amazement;
Scarce was there a sound
As Jesus went up and touched the coffin;
Those carrying it seemed rooted to the ground.

They stood motionless when Jesus spoke
"Young man I say to you arise."
The dead man sat up and began to talk
Wonderment filled everyone's eyes!

The people spontaneously praised God
But so many remained afraid
As they said a great prophet has come among us
One who has clearly come to our aid.

The widow one moment in total sadness
Facing a life of utter despair
Must have now rejoiced with the others
In spreading the good news of Jesus everywhere.

Lord we want to spread the good news
Of the widow who regained her son
How we want to tell everyone
Of the wonderful things Jesus has done.

# JESUS ANOINTED BY A SINFUL WOMAN
(Based on Luke 7:36–50)

Jesus is invited, by Simon the Pharisee, to dinner. There would be many guests there who would have been offered the usual hospitality but somehow the most important guest of all is overlooked! A rich household, as this undoubtedly was, would have a number of servants whose duties would include washing and drying the feet of all guests before they entered the main part of the house.

Perhaps Simon was so overwhelmed when Jesus arrived that all normal hospitality was somehow forgotten. Soon our Lord was reclining at the table and before he was really settled He was confronted with the town harlot!

Jesus would be somewhat taken aback but Simon would be completely floored. This was not part of the plan at all! How did she get in? Perhaps the door was left open for the many guests scheduled to come and she had slipped in quietly unnoticed. Somehow she had found out that Jesus was having dinner at the Pharisee's house.

Perhaps their eyes had met earlier as Jesus made his way towards his appointment. Maybe some words had been exchanged as she stood in her customary position on the street corner. She couldn't forget that look of love in His eyes as the distance between them extended. More than likely she went home changed her clothing and then made her mind up to find Him at all costs. The pain of her existence, the life she was living only served to quicken her steps to find Jesus.

At last she finds out where He is and soon she is stood behind Him. She collapses raining down tears on His feet. Then she wipes them with her hair, kisses them and anoints them with fragrant oil.

This is an extraordinary act of selfless love to our Lord. She takes upon herself all the heat and filth of the animal infested streets of the day and washes it away not with water from a jar but with the tears of repentance for her sinful life. Then after drying pours the most precious thing she has lavishly on Him. She was offering the whole of her past life to the only One who could give her new life and by pouring out her all on His feet surely she was saying to herself from now on I want to walk only in Your ways. This really was an occasion where actions speak louder than words!

Simon was still quietly fuming. He couldn't take it in that Jesus should allow this to happen to Him. Wasn't He a prophet after all, he was thinking to himself.

Jesus knew what was running through his mind so He told him a story. "Two men owed money to a certain money-lender. One owed him five hundred denari and the other fifty. Neither of them had the money to pay him back, so he cancelled the debts of both. Now which of them will love him more?"

Simon replied, "I suppose the one who had the bigger debt cancelled."

"You have judged correctly," Jesus said.

In his embarrassment at the woman's presence Simon was quick to judge her. She had come along and spoilt his party. Simon's debt was being called into account here – the woman's was forgiven and forgotten. Jesus reminded Simon that when He came he hadn't given Him any water for His feet nor kissed Him as the custom was. In sharp contrast the woman it could be said had gone overboard with her affections.

Jesus said to her: "Your sins are forgiven." In her great love so freely given and lavished on our Lord we see the gratitude vividly portrayed of the one who is forgiven. Perhaps the moment when their eyes met in the street she knew she was forgiven. The look of love in Jesus' eyes resulted in this lavish display of affection by a woman who had perhaps never experienced any love in her life before. This could well have resulted in her living the life she did but no more – it only took one look and the whole picture changed.

There is no better time to look in the Saviour's direction than right now. We mistakenly think we have to put several things right ourselves, then we can come to Him. He just wants us to come just as we are!

There was an opportunity for the other guests there to put their lives right. They, however, could only say among themselves: "Who is this who even forgives sin." They looked at the woman – but couldn't see themselves as they really were. They wouldn't understand when Jesus then said to her: "Your faith has saved you, go in peace."

Jesus had said earlier: "He who has been forgiven little loves little." The tragedy for so many there was that they didn't even see their need for forgiveness. Simon's blindness to the Kingdom of Heaven was only highlighted by the actions of the woman who wonderfully received forgiveness. There is no record in this account of Simon even asking Jesus to forgive him for not providing the basic hospitality which would have been offered to the other guests. If he had maybe we wouldn't have had this wonderful story handed down to us!

How Jesus' heart must have ached not only for this Pharisee but all the other guests present at the dinner.

# AT THE HOUSE OF SIMON
### (Based on Luke 7:44-48)

"I entered your house dear Simon
What did you offer to Me?"
Then Jesus turned towards the woman
"Look at her, what do you see?
I came in with dusty, dirty feet;
Of them you seemed unaware
But she has washed My feet with her tears
And dried them with her hair.

You gave Me no kiss of welcome
But she, her joy was complete;
From the moment I first entered
She has not stopped kissing My feet.
You gave Me no oil for My head
When I entered your room
But she has anointed My feet
With a jar of precious perfume.

Dear Simon you cannot have failed
To notice her loving touch.
Her sins, and they are many, are forgiven
Because she loved so much.
The man who has little to be forgiven
Has only a little love to give.
Simon, dear Simon, where are you?
Look again and start to live."

# "BRING THE BOY TO ME"

What a difference a day makes for our Saviour. One day in His transfigured form He is talking to Elijah and Moses on the mountain then the next after leaving it He is approached by a pleading father whose son is possessed by an evil spirit. What a contrast indeed!

Jesus could have been forgiven if His mind was like ours. Our heads would still be in the clouds if we had been there with those three disciples. Back to earth with a bang we could say but our Saviour's mind was immediately focused on what was around him. Even though the man was in a crowd Jesus heard him and immediately responded by saying "bring the boy to me." Could we expect anything less from our Saviour who always responded to the needs presented to Him.

"How long has he been like this?" You can almost feel the compassion flowing through our Saviour's veins as He enquired of his father. This could only have been enhanced when the Father told him since childhood. What suffering his father and presumably his mother have gone through?

The father is desperate: "if you can do anything..." The years have taken away what little expectation there was regarding their son. Even the smallest improvement would be so welcome. "Everything is possible for him who believes." Jesus' words hit the poor father where he was. He doesn't believe much can happen for his son but acknowledges this by saying "I do believe; help me overcome my unbelief!" Jesus, often faced with hypocrisy, must have inwardly smiled and perhaps rejoiced at the man's honesty and so wonderfully answered the cries of his heart.

The father's expectations were soon to be greatly exceeded!

Jesus commanded the deaf and mute spirit to come out of him and furthermore commanded it never to enter him again.

When everyone thought the boy was dead, Jesus took him by the hand and lifted him to his feet and he stood up. Jesus gave him back to his grateful father.

What celebrations there would be at home that evening. All the family would gather hardly able to believe their eyes. The boy was totally free and like our Saviour the previous day his appearance was changed. Of course there was a difference but we know that when we have truly met with God we are changed not only inwardly but outwardly.

All the people were amazed at the greatness of God. None more so than one extremely grateful father who has just received a new son.

# THE HEALING OF A BOY WITH AN EVIL SPIRIT
## (Based on Luke 9:37-43)

From the mountainside
They came down the next day
A large crowd was there to meet them
So blocking Jesus and the disciples' way.

"Teacher, take a look at my son.
He is my only child.
One minute he is quite normal
The next uncontrollably wild."

"Lord this wild spirit is killing him."
You can almost hear the father's plea.
"I begged your disciples to drive it out
But they couldn't help me."

Jesus' annoyance with His disciples
Was soon forgotten in compassion for the boy,
The father's awful pain was soon to be over
To be replaced by great joy.

"Bring your son here," Jesus said.
The boy made his way through the crowd
As he did so Satan attacked him
From the ground he screamed out loud.

At the height of his convulsions
Jesus wonderfully stepped in
To heal the boy and return him to his father
So together new life could begin.

Like the prodigal in the story
The father's joy was unconfined.
How wonderful to have your son back
Healed in body, soul and mind.

Lord we thank You for Your great mercy
That reaches out to every soul
Your only desire for us is that
We be made completely whole.

So with the people there
We truly stand amazed
At Your greatness and goodness;
Father in Heaven be praised.

# HEALING ON THE SABBATH

Can we imagine the suffering this woman had gone through just to get to the synagogue? Each week, perhaps more often, she made the journey and every time it would get harder. She can barely remember the day when she was upright and free of pain. Just getting her clothes on to get ready to go was agony itself and then it was some walk to the synagogue. She was determined however. Giving up was not in her make-up.

She had heard that this Jesus was teaching that day. She specially wanted to be there. Word had got about that He was a prophet and spoke with such authority.

She made her way to her seat and was listening intently. Suddenly Jesus stopped teaching. He noticed her. Maybe He had seen her many times before but His Father made Him especially aware of her this day.

Jesus called her forward and said to her, "Woman, you are set free from your infirmity." Then He put His hands on her and immediately she straightened up and praised God.

She couldn't believe it. Eighteen years of suffering at the hands of Satan and now she was instantly healed. How she praised God. I am sure she just wanted to run around the synagogue so everyone could see her. How wonderful for her as she could now look in everyone's face with no effort at all.

Satan was however ready to deal out the last card in his hand in the shape of the synagogue ruler, who said to the people: "There are six days for work. So come and be healed on those days, not on the Sabbath."

How sad that this ruler could not share the joy of the woman and the joy of so many others there. He was so tied up with the rules and regulations of the day that he missed out on what really mattered. God had visited His people!

The Lord was not slow in answering him – and the ones who were similarly bound up. "You hypocrites! Doesn't each of you on the Sabbath untie his ox or donkey from the stall and lead it out to give it water? Then should not this woman, a daughter of Abraham, whom Satan has kept bound for eighteen long years, be set free on the Sabbath Day from what bound her?"

The people waited expectantly for some answer from this official. The eyes of everyone are on him and all ears await his reply. But there is just silence. How many times did our Lord with a word or sometimes a look just silence the accuser.

His opponents suffered another humiliation that day but the people rejoiced. How delighted they were with all the wonderful things He was doing. None more so than this daughter of Abraham who is now able to do something she hasn't been able to do for a long, long time – turn her eyes and her heart to heaven. She must have felt ten feet tall.

We cannot imagine ourselves having the attitude of that synagogue ruler, but it is so easy for us to let things get in the way which then prevent us from seeing what God is really doing not only in our own lives but in the lives of others. We may not be bent over as that woman was but sadly so many of us only have limited vision.

In future may our hearts always be open to the supernatural movement of God. He is after all a Heavenly Father who takes a delight in showering us with His blessings.

\*\*\*\*\*\*

# HEALING ON THE SABBATH
(Based on Luke 13:10-17)

Crippled by a spirit this dear woman
For over eighteen years.
We can only imagine her pain
And her lonely tears.

She shuffles round the synagogue
Trying her best not to fall
She who was so bent over
She couldn't straighten up at all.

Her heart must have leapt within her
"Is Jesus calling me?"
Soon she was there in front of Him
One minute infirm the next set free.

"You are set free from your infirmity"
Were the words Jesus said.
Then with loving compassion
He placed His hands on her head.

Immediately she straightened up;
Her vertebrae just falling into place.
She looked up and then she beheld
The Master's glorious face.

No longer were her eyes sentenced
To look only at the floor.
She could now look up
To Him who we adore.

All the people were delighted
With the wonderful things He was doing
And especially now before their eyes
At this daughter of Abraham's renewing.

# I WANT TO SEE

Jesus came to the outskirts of Jericho on His way up to Jerusalem. A large crowd was with Him noisily chatting together and no doubt going over all the wonderful things they had seen and heard our Saviour do.

By the roadside in his accustomed spot was Bartimaeus begging from all who passed by. We know nothing of this man but we can assume that he has been blind for a long time and that sadly his little space beside the road had become his home as well. He had something in common with Jesus in that like the Son of Man 'he had no place to lay his head'. The trodden in ground his bed and a stone his pillow. Perhaps he had in his earlier days enjoyed the comforts of home but like His Master there was a time when home had to be left behind. There the similarity ends.

Bartimaeus heard the rustle of the crowd and asked what was going on.

Jesus of Nazareth was going by he was told. He had heard of this Jesus all right and saw in Him someone who really could help him. The noise of the crowd was very loud now to his sensitive ears. At the top of his voice he yelled out, "Jesus, Son of David, have mercy on me!" There was a real sense of desperation in his voice.

Those ahead of Jesus told the man to shut up, but he only yelled all the louder, "Son of David, mercy, have mercy on me!"

Jesus stopped and ordered the man to be brought over to Him. When he had come near, Jesus asked, "What do you want from Me?"

Our Lord's question to Bartimaeus would seem to be superfluous. There was no doubt that Jesus could see that there before Him was a blind man living a wretched lifestyle. Anyone could see that. It is true to say, however, that some people have got so used to living in a certain way that they would feel threatened by a change that may well require them to stand on their own two feet. This would clearly not seem to be the case with our blind friend but for some reason best known of course to our Saviour He posed the question to him.

Bartimaeus' reply was immediate, "Lord, I want to see."

Jesus said to him, "Receive your sight; your faith has healed you." Immediately he received his sight and followed Jesus, praising God. When all the people saw it, they also praised God.

I wonder how long Bartimaeus followed Jesus? Did he become a true follower of His? Was the healing he received part of a greater healing? Did he come to know Jesus as Lord and Saviour? That is the greatest healing of all.

# I WANT TO SEE
(Based on Luke 18:35-43 & Mark 10:46-52)

He was sitting by the roadside begging
In the scorching heat of the day,
When to his delight he heard
That Jesus was coming his way.

He could not let this opportunity pass;
This was his one chance to see.
He shouted "Jesus, Son of David
Have mercy on me."

The people told him to be quiet
But he shouted all the more.
Those heartfelt cries of Bartimaeus
Jesus just couldn't ignore.

Jesus asked the crowd to call him
"Cheer up," they said, "get on your feet."
Bartimaeus without hesitation rushed towards Jesus
His joy was soon to be complete.

Jesus asked him what he wanted
To cause his heart to delight
Bartimaeus could have wanted something
Other than to receive his sight.

"I want to see" the voice rang out
From the blind man's troubled breast
"Go," said Jesus, "your faith has healed you."
Immediately he could see and followed the rest.

How wonderful it is to meet with Jesus.
The blind man's joy was unconfined.
Oh what joy there is when you receive
Healing of body, soul and mind.

How the people praised God
For what they saw that day.
Let us continue to give Him thanks
As we faithfully walk in His way.

So many people are thankful to receive a touch from the Master, which transforms them outwardly, but no inner change takes place at all.

Only a matter of days earlier Jesus had been travelling along the border between Samaria and Galilee. On entering a village, He was met with ten men who had leprosy. They cried out to Him, "Jesus, Master, have pit on us." When He saw them, He said, "Go show yourselves to the priests." It was the priests' job to pronounce that people were clean as a prelude to their taking up normal life again. There was such fear among everyone of leprosy and its manifestations.

Significantly Jesus did not say "You are healed now go and show yourselves to the priests."

As soon as one of them saw he was healed he turned around and came back praising God in a loud voice. He threw himself at Jesus' feet and thanked Him – and he was a Samaritan!

How often Jesus must have felt saddened and disillusioned with His own people. Could it be that the only Samaritan among the ten who were healed was the one who came back to thank Him. This would not be inconsistent with other stories in the Bible.

Jesus said, "Were not ten healed? Where are the other nine? Can none be found to come back and give glory to God except this outsider?" Then He said to him, "Get up. On your way. Your faith has healed and saved you."

Only one out of the ten secured a place in the Kingdom of Heaven. How heartbroken Jesus must have been! Our Lord offers the Gift of Life – Eternal Life to everyone but sadly too many people are happy to receive the gift but not the Giver.

We are living in exciting times where the Giver of Life is showing Himself in so many different ways. There is no time like the present to just come to Him. He will not only cure your blindness but also open your eyes so that you will see as you have never seen before!

# TEN HEALED - ONE SAVED
(Based on Luke 17:11-19)

Jesus travelled along the border
Between Samaria and Galilee that day.
Into a village he went
Heading the Jerusalem way.

On entering the village itself
He was met by ten men in real need.
They were lepers who on seeing the Master
Began to earnestly plead.

"Jesus, Master, have pity on us,"
Was their single cry.
They knew that without His help
They would surely die.

Jesus had such compassion for them.
Leprosy was such a terrible disease.
He took a good look at them
And just wanted to put them at ease.

"Go, show yourselves to the priests."
They would know what this could mean
So they went and while on their way
They were all made clean!

What joy must have been in their hearts
They certainly had cause to rejoice
But sadly only one of them came back
Praising God in a loud voice.

He threw himself at Jesus' feet
So thankful was this man
What pain for the Master – only one returning
And he a Samaritan!

What of His fellow countrymen
Those He would say are Mine.
How sad the heart of the Saviour
When He said, "Where are the nine?"

Just the outsider came back of the ten,
For Jesus what agony of soul.
It was only to the grateful heart could He say
"Your faith has made you whole."

What a thankful people we should be
Always maintaining a positive attitude
A people who continually overflow
With hearts of overwhelming gratitude.

# JESUS AND THE TAX COLLECTOR
(Based on Luke 19:1-10)

Jesus entered Jericho, a lush area where the first fruits and the best are grown. It would also be a lush centre of taxation.

Jesus was only passing through but one man was determined to meet up with Him. His name was Zacchaeus who had risen through the ranks to become a chief tax collector. He had one disadvantage, which he had spent his life over-compensating for – he was small in stature. He couldn't see over the crowd and no one would be kindly disposed to let him through.

He decided to sacrifice his position and the dignity that went with it to go on ahead and climb a tree so he could see Jesus as He went by.

As he was up there he perhaps reflected on his life. He had power and wealth but little else. Disliked by the Romans who employed him and even more so by his own people who received little mercy at his hands, his only friends were fellow tax collectors and prostitutes. These two groups were treated as outcasts of society. He couldn't walk anywhere without being recognised and derided by his fellow Jews.

Zacchaeus must have heard stories about this Jesus and that He was a friend of tax collectors. I could do with a friend thought Zacchaeus – a real friend! He must have heard how Levi's life had been changed – how he left everything and followed Him. Yes I must meet this Jesus.

As the noise of the crowd increases so does the desperation in the tax collector's heart. I can't go on living like this. The money meant a lot and the position at one time – but now........

Suddenly Jesus stopped below the tree and looked up then said: "Zacchaeus hurry down, I must stay at your house today," Zacchaeus, in a state of complete shock, scrambled out of the tree to the ground hardly able to take in what had just been said to him.

He immediately took Jesus to his home probably pinching himself all the way there!

The tax collector was indeed shocked that Jesus wanted to go to his house but so were the people who voiced their disapproval with I am sure at least a hint of jealousy. "He has gone to be the guest of a sinner!" they exclaimed.

The people were in for a further shock as Zacchaeus stood up and said to the Lord, in their hearing, "Master, here and now I give half of my possessions to the poor, and if I have cheated anybody out of anything, I will pay back four times the amount."

A miracle has occurred – a camel has passed through the eye of a needle – for this man was rich. The rich young ruler turned away as many have before and since. Not so Zacchaeus for he had come to the end of himself and in Jesus' acceptance of him the floodgates of repentance were opened.

Jesus could indeed say: "Salvation has come to this house." It had and as the days and weeks went by this man of small stature would become a giant in the community as he sought to meet the needs of the poor with a now generous heart and also to pay back those he had cheated.

Jesus is still seeking out people who are prepared to invest in His Kingdom.

Deep down I know that as I continue to try and put You first in everything then my stature will grow. Please help me to realise that the only worthwhile investment I should make is for eternity's sake.

\*\*\*\*\*\*

# TODAY SALVATION HAS COME TO THIS HOUSE
(Luke 19:9)

How could Zacchaeus give as he did?
It was that his eyes were no longer dim.
He had hoarded for decades
But now salvation had come to him.

He yielded not because it was easy;
Something happened within.
It was not that he had cried and prayed
And then with a tremendous struggle given in.

His response was immediate, he did not surrender
A bit today then a bit tomorrow,
Until he was forced finally to surrender all,
As though with regret and much sorrow.

He had fallen into great disrepute
In order that his money may grow;
Because God brought salvation to his house
He let it all go.

# THE PARABLE OF THE LOST SON

After returning home from a week's holiday in the Yorkshire Dales in the summer of 1986, the above parable came alive for me. I wonder how many millions of people down the years have been wonderfully transformed by this story.

My wife Alison certainly had needed the break perhaps more than I did. For a number of years I had suffered with ulcerative colitis. The severity of it at times rendering me to periods of incontinence at worse and a general feeling of weakness at best. Always there was that uncertainty within me whenever we did anything or went anywhere: "would I be alright?" .

I became a Christian in 1978 and this followed by a wonderful personal experience of God in February 1980, in which I was baptised in the Holy Spirit, certainly helped me cope with my problem.

Ulcerative colitis is an extremely selfish illness which makes one continually think about oneself when of course the reality of the Christian faith is quite the contrary.

We had stayed at a lovely farmhouse in a small village with a total population of just eighteen. One night a man who was living there for a time after getting over a divorce and the loss of his position as a Minister in a small church said something to me that really pulled me up short. "If you don't watch it you're going to lose your marriage like I lost mine." I was stunned but took his words to heart and began to look at my life in a more realistic way. I was going through it with my condition but what of my wife? His words to me made me realise that in all this I had in truth become almost unaware of how much she was suffering not only with all the extra work she had to do but seeing me and experiencing me as I was.

A few days later we returned home from the holiday and immediately I sought out Barrie our Minister. I was sorely troubled and just the thought that there was some truth in what had been said to me alarmed me considerably. I loved my wife to whom I had been married for twenty years and any threat to the marriage had to be treated seriously. It was a warning to me, I knew that.

Barrie and I met together and we shared and he prayed for me and then read out the story of the Prodigal Son.

Before he began to read I was reflecting how I really was. I felt as though there was a brick wall in front of me and a brick wall behind me. I was stuck. I couldn't go forward and I couldn't go back.

Barrie concluded his reading at Verse 24 of Luke 15 but it was verse 20 that completely changed me.

"But while he was still a long way off, his father saw him and was filled with compassion for him;  he ran to his son, threw his arms around him and kissed him."

It was those last few words **"threw his arms around him and kissed him"**.  Suddenly the two walls lifted and I was free.  I felt totally loved by my Heavenly Father.  Sadly I had known little love from my earthly father particularly from the age of twelve when my parents were divorced.  The reading of this scripture brought great healing into my life and today I feel just the same – totally loved by my Heavenly Father.

Returning to the story of the Lost Son, we aren't really sure why the younger son left home. It may well have been as much the attitude of his older brother that made him long to get away, as his desire for fame and fortune. It could just be that his father expected too much of him or had a relationship with him rather like Jacob had with Joseph.  One thing for sure was that his leaving home would not have been a quick decision.  He knew that as things stood if he left home it was for good.  Jewish tradition had it that such a thing was just not done.  Everyone of course in the area would know when he departed.  How must his father have felt when he left?  He didn't expect to ever see him again but he didn't have to wait as long as Jacob!  Father and son were reunited before too long and what a reunion it was.  A picture of heaven perhaps!

Reflecting on all of this I recently wrote a poem, "THE HOMECOMING", written as though I were that wayward son.

# THE HOMECOMING
(Based on Luke 15:11-24)

I will arise and go to my father
You could say sanity has come at last.
How I long for the security of home
And to relive the good times past.

I so much wanted to leave home
For I felt I had so much to learn
Of the world and its ways
But now I just long to return.

Will my father take me back?
What words can I find to say
To explain to my dear father
Why I acted in this way?

What will he think when he sees me
In such an awful state?
Just the thought of that
Would make anyone hesitate.

I must go back though
And face my father's wrath.
I can expect no other reaction for I
Have strayed far away from the path.

I will go and plead with him.
Perhaps he will understand.
Maybe he will take me on
To work as a hired hand.

I have been walking several days
And now within me is a feeling of alarm
For I can see in the distance
Just the outline of my father's farm.

Can I even expect to be received?
Thoughts consume me like when and how.
Yet I've come so far I must continue
I can't run away now.

As I draw closer to my amazement
I see a figure running towards me.
My eyes well up, my senses revive
Is it?  Surely it cannot be.

Suddenly I know, I recognise
There is no mistaking that face
All fears are gone and suddenly
I am locked in my father's embrace.

My words of explanation go unheeded
Speaking as an unworthy son
For love so beautifully overrides
All the terrible things I have done.

Overwhelmed with His love
At His feet I now fall.
I am forgiven, I am accepted
By the Greatest Father of All.

# MOORLEY'S

*We are growing publishers, adding several new titles to our list each year. We also undertake private publications and commissioned works.*

Our range of publications includes:

**Books of Verse:**
Devotional Poetry
Recitations
**Drama**
Bible Plays
Sketches
Nativity Plays
Passiontide Plays
Easter Plays
Demonstrations
**Resource Books**
Assembly Material
Songs and Musicals
Children's Addresses
Prayers and Graces
Daily Readings
Books for Speakers
**Activity Books**
Quizzes
Puzzles
Painting Books
**Church Stationery**
Notice Books
Cradle Rolls
Hymn Board Numbers

Please send a stamped addressed envelope (approx. 9" x 6") for the current catalogue or consult your local Christian Bookshop who should stock or be able to order our titles.